Alzheimer's: Beyond Caregiving

Miki Klocke

for Mom

In the beginning ...

Numbness from the diagnosis began to ebb. I said to my neighbor, "I don't know what all this means. Where do I start?"

Her gardener's father-in-law had Alzheimer's. She asked his wife to reach out.

The call came. I couldn't speak. I shattered into a million pieces—confusion, helplessness, despair, all colliding. And overwhelming fear.

This stranger understood.

As a seasoned caregiver she listened to my tears. It was the permission I needed to feel the crash of conflicting emotions—to grieve, not only for my mom, but for me, for the life I thought I would live.

At 33 years old, newly single and hungry for a life of adventure, I had fallen into an abyss—the lonely world of an Alzheimer's caregiver.

And so the journey began ...

In those early stages of Mom's disease, I would never have thought it possible to find anything good. Contentment was preposterous.

Yet the thoughts expressed in this book kept surfacing. It took 15 years for them to coalesce, buried beneath the rubble of my derailed life.

I became a wanderer in the Land of Inbetweendom ...

Every caregiver's experience is unique, a universe known only to that person. But we share feelings others may not understand, feelings we find hard to express, feelings tinged with the shame of being lost.

The advice became cliché—find time for yourself. There isn't any. What we do find is what is within us. For a decade what I found was depression, inadequacy, anger and resentment.

Loneliness was the price of taking care of Mom, that was my conclusion.

I found another way ...

Now I know there is a way to live that opens me to peace. I hope my story will resonate with your own, and that you will look again at what is within, and find your way to contentment, maybe even your own peace.

I learned to stop gritting my teeth ...

Mine was a single mom who raised two daughters and worked two jobs. Yet she made sure we had the best life has to offer—family gatherings, girl scouting, music, camping. Mom taught us the rewards of hard work, the freedom to dream.

Those values and experiences shaped me growing up. Alzheimer's didn't end Mom's lessons. She had been here all along, if only I had listened. This time she wasn't teaching me about the world outside, but the one within, the one I needed to inhabit to survive and find my way as her caregiver.

A new reality emerged ...

Rather than the vapor trail from a jet overhead, Mom would see a train. I would correct her each time, to no avail. Then I remembered she had grown up in a small town. A train pulling into the station was a big deal, cause for excitement. While I saw air, she felt a thrill.

We no longer shared the most basic understanding that links people. And we never would again. Accepting the brutal truth of Alzheimer's freed me from fighting a losing battle.

That milestone moment was a breakthrough ...

The barrier between me and Mom began to crumble. We didn't have to share the same reality to experience a connection, our bond as mother and daughter. We could share affection. It was mine to give, and to receive.

I found my way back to Mom ...

I learned to recognize those precious moments, feelings binding us where a shared reality could not.

For too long such opportunities had been crushed by my refusal to see them.

For a decade I saw only loss—my job, my freedom, my dreams. I didn't understand why Mom's friends and family had deserted us. Why some of mine did. Irritation and the underlying loss behind it filled me.

I found my way back to me, a new me ...

The disease had robbed Mom of precious memories. It hadn't robbed me. What it did rob me of was my desire and willingness to feel.

In resisting the pain of loss, I had shut myself off to feeling everything else along with it.

I felt isolated...

Mom was free of disappointment in people who couldn't handle her disease. I wasn't.

It was up to me to nurture relationships with those who understood my limited freedom.

I learned to be a better friend, to accept that we each share responsibility to make an effort.

My isolation had been self-imposed, that abyss of loneliness where the future holds nothing good ...

I started taking Mom out for a meal. At the restaurant, she would thank everyone in a loud voice. At first I was embarrassed.

Yet I never saw one person who didn't smile in response. Mom was grateful for her food, for being out, for me...whatever it was.

I learned the power of gratitude. Mom's behavior had changed, but her core values remained.

Ten years later I learned new lessons from Mom ...

Crows would caw. Mom would say they were happy, or upset, or some other emotion. Birds weren't separate from us.

We are all different and yet all participants in the same world.

Mom worked her entire adult life. Alzheimer's reduced her abilities to yard work; picking up acorns.

But that was enough for Mom. She wanted to help, to contribute to a joint effort.

My vision cleared ...

I began to look for the feeling beneath Mom's actions rather than the ability to follow through.

I saw Mom differently.

She still had the same need she'd always had—to be included, to matter, the same as me, and most of us. In that way, she was still here.

Mom dreamed of all the places she
would travel in her retirement ...

There is no retirement with Alzheimer's.

But I still had my dreams. Slowly I began to re-envision them. All the things I wanted in life were still there.

They just hadn't been realized the way I had imagined. The way they would have when I believed I was in control.

It wasn't the world that had to change. It was me.

The biggest lesson was the hardest to learn—control is an illusion ...

Alzheimer's throws caregivers into an out-of-control world where everything is distorted. I saw offers of help as a reflection of inadequacy, and declined.

A decade later I understood that control is an illusion, that I did need help, that offers had been sincere.

Hanging on to the myth of control had led to my captivity. Pride and independence had isolated me, not the disease, not taking care of Mom.

A new life awaited me ...

After a decade I began climbing out of the abyss, shedding resentment—disappointment in friends and family, sadness over dashed hopes.

I began the long walk back, not to the world I had known and grieved over, but a different one where I saw hope and possibilities.

What I discovered in this new world ...

Caring for Mom had given me
something I might never have had.

I found strength, the capacity to feel
love in the most difficult
circumstances, a willingness to let in
all that life has to offer, bad and good.

My senses opened ...

Now I hear squirrels chatter, feel
the wind, smell the sea. I look
around and let my imagination
run wild—the clouds are sharks
swimming in a sea of
pink—shape, form, color, texture,
beauty I never dreamed was
right before my eyes.

Learning to let go of expectations
that she would have the future
she dreamed of, that I would,
took a long time.

I don't look back with regret
at those years I was lost ...

They weren't wasted. I was forging a new me. The old me couldn't have found precious moments, shared affection, or honored childhood memories, caring for Mom.

Instead of the numb and closed off woman I might have become, I am embracing life in a whole new way. I travel when I can get away, take day trips, say yes to opportunities. If a friend invites me to dinner, I go. If I want to walk on the beach, I do. If I want to streak my hair purple just to be me, I can.

Distractions tug at me, what I need to do today, tomorrow, next week. After 15 years with no time for myself, the freedom to react to what I feel, what I need, is like waking from a long exhausting sleep.

In letting go, I found my freedom. I found myself. I found pure love.

love is more than a memory
it lives in the heart
it is rooted in our being
it is the earth and sky
blowing in the wind
the warmth of the sun
the cool of shade
it is the key
that opens the door
to the home within us

Our journey together ended on June 27th, 2017. But our story lives on in my mind, in my heart, in my soul.

Acknowledgements

I owe a debt of gratitude to Lori Windsor Mohr for her editorial talent and for encouraging me to tell this story from the inside out.

Many thanks to Mary Ogle for her graphic design skills.

I also give much gratitude to the Alzheimer's Association/ HELP of Ojai California chapter Caregivers Support Group. Without this group our journey would not have been possible.

I appreciate and have great respect for Dr. Frecker M.D., the only neurologist in a long search who would look Mom in the eye and direct questions to her.

References

Miki Klocke
mikiklocke.com

Lori Mohr
loriwindsormohr@gmail.com
The Road at my Door
- available on Amazon

Mary Ogle
maryogle.com

Alzheimer's Association
alz.org

Join me on Instagram (@AlzStories) to share your own journey. We connect through stories. Sharing our fears and vulnerabilities opens our hearts to love and gives us the courage to continue on our path.

My ultimate hope for this book is that it be available for free to any and all caregivers of those with Alzheimer's disease. You can help make that happen by purchasing 50 or more books at a discounted bulk rate and donate them to your local caregiver support groups, doctor's offices or senior centers. I will add a sticker to those specific books acknowledging your donation. They may include an "in memory of" or "dedicated to" if you so choose. Please contact me for more information.

Miki@MikiKlocke.com

When you need a time-out, a mini-mind vacation or a few laughs check out my gift book titles. Show them to your loved ones, you may discover an opportunity to laugh together or tap into a long term memory. No shared reality required.

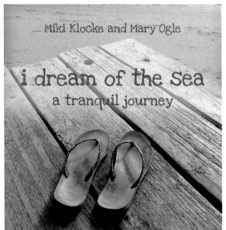

Available on Amazon.com

Miki Klocke is a photographer and author. Her images mirror what is going on in her heart and soul. During her 17 years of taking care of her mom, her images reflect a lonely time, an introspective time, a longing for peace and solitude.....

copyright ©Miki Klocke 907 press

Printed in the United States of America

First Printing 2017

ISBN: 978-0692961148

Made in the USA
Las Vegas, NV
18 July 2021

26671280R00038